RED VELVET FOREST

Red Velvet Forest

SHAWNA LEMAY

The Muses' Company Series Editor: Clarise Foster
Cover art by Robert Lemay
Book design by Terry Gallagher/Doowah Design Inc.
Author photo by Robert Lemay
Printed and bound in Canada on 100% post-consumer recycled paper.

We acknowledge the financial support of the Manitoba Arts Council, The Canada Council for the Arts and the Government of Canada through the Book Publishing Industry Development Program (BPIDP) for our publishing program.

Library and Archives Canada Cataloguing in Publication

Lemay, Shawna, 1966-
Red velvet forest / Shawna Lemay.

Poems.
ISBN 978-1-897289-40-2

I. Title.

PS8573.E5358R42 2009 C811'.54 C2009-901262-6

J. Gordon Shillingford Publishing
P.O. Box 86, RPO Corydon Avenue, Winnipeg, MB Canada R3M 3S3

for Rob and Chloe

Life is red, it is many colours.

—Gwendolyn MacEwen

Fire, we think, marvelous fire, everything starts in fire.

—Charles Wright

I want to say words that flame
as I say them, but I keep quiet and don't try
to make both worlds fit in one mouthful.

—Rumi

You will find more in forests than in books;
trees and rocks will teach you things
no master can make known to you.

Bernard of Clairvaux

In this world of ours we must burn completely.
Each of us must resolve himself completely in the flames,
in the resolution that belongs to him alone.

—Juan Ramon Jimenez

It's not having what you want,
it's wanting what you've got.

—Sheryl Crow

I dedicate myself to the color red,
very scarlet, like this blood of mine…

—Clarice Lispector

Acknowledgements

Red Velvet Forest began as the creative thesis to my MA in English at the University of Alberta. I would like to gratefully acknowledge the wonderful support, advice, and encouragement of Bert Almon who supervised the thesis. Thanks also to Patricia Demers, Ted Bishop, John Considine, and Greg Hollingshead, the professors of the courses I took during my M.A. Much of what I learned in their classes has filtered into these poems. Thank you to the readers on my committee, Douglas Barbour and Don Kuiken. The following friends were indispensable in the writing of this manuscript: Annette Schouten Woudstra, Barbara Langhorst and Lee Elliott. Many thanks also to Olga Costopoulos, Michael Penny, Iman Mersal, Kimmy Beach. Thank you to my parents and to my mother-in-law. The biggest thanks goes to Rob and our daughter, Chloe Lemay.

Most of the last section of this book appeared as a chapbook produced by the Olive Reading Series.

This book wouldn't exist if Clarise Foster hadn't believed in the work. I'm grateful for her nuanced and careful editing and deep understanding of the poems. Thanks to The Muses' Company for everything and all...

Table of Contents

The Circumference

Disgrace / 17

The Dead Matter / 18

One Night / 20

Invisible, Unfinished / 22

Alone, Alone, Alone, Together / 24

It Makes Sense / 25

Curlicues / 27

I'm Tired of Being Summoned / 29

This Time / 31

Solitude and Return / 32

Feeding the Path / 34

A Frail Clarity / 35

Called Away / 36

Thin-Skinned / 37

Why Not / 38

I've Let Myself Go / 40

Blue Girl / 41

Subterraneous Re-enchantment / 43

Salt / 45

A Black Horse Running After / 47

Leaving the Room / 49

Lost

Reversal / 53
Apparition of the Clearing / 55
Talisman / 56
Assassination Plot / 58
Doing Other / 59
The Rain is Unromantic / 61
Falling Short / 62
But the Gods are Organized / 64
Lost / 66
The Extremities of an Innocence / 68
Reminder / 70
Blundering Reconciliations / 71
All Manner of Things / 72
Possible Gods / 73
Sway / 75
Dream Stumbling / 78
The Voices Culminate / 80

Red Velvet Forest

Dream of the Red Forest / 87
Velvet Fire, Tranquil Blue / 90
Insomnia Diary / 92
The Forest of Disappearance / 95
Burning Forest / 97
The Red Tree, My Heart / 98
Red / 100
Circling the Forest / 101
The Azure-Vermillion Tangle / 103
Red Velvet / 105
A Way of Meeting / 107
Want / 108

Dragonsblood Red / 110
To the Wolf / 111
A Third / 113
Sorrow, at Last, Failure. Joy. / 115
Woodcutter in the Forest / 117

When I was the Forest—essay / 119

Notes / 125
Bibliography / 127

The Circumference

Disgrace

The circumference.
What am I doing here?
How does it happen?
I am
expelled.
I am at the edge of the forest in spring snow I am
a torture.
I canter, foaming, the bit in my teeth
almost know freedom
the way back in.
I forget.

You've got to fall in love with me here once.
Again.
See?

But no one falls in love with this.
Just as no one takes the photograph of me that I want.
With just the right one everything would change
I would be known.
I yearn for the invisibility of being known.

I'll settle for indifference.
I don't spare myself from remembering
every instance of acting the fool
mouth full of the twisted, the deformed.

I find a book I wrote hanging inside someone's garbage pail.
It doesn't hurt me.

From the writhing core of humiliation
one night, in the middle
I learn not to disturb.
I'm quiet. I proceed.

I'm at the circumference.
It's no disgrace.

The Dead Matter

It's early.
The dead matter has been cleared
from the almost living.
Poppies and lady's mantle begin to frill the earth.
The trees have buds
but winter has knotted its fingers
around my heart so long now
I can't believe they'll unfurl—leaves or fingers.
I don't know anything about prayer
so I waste time praying for the leaves.
Who knows why winter will return sometimes in spring.

Half the year, more, is lived in white
making green pictures up in the mind.
Green pastures, thickening into forests.
By the time the snow melts, the underbrush has you.

The dead season has that effect.
chokes you with your own imagination.
Scrapes your cheeks and every dark turn
threatens your eyes, bleeds your ankles.

No wonder I can scarcely keep my eyes open
in the blinding.
Yesterday I clawed decaying leaves
severed dead limbs
gathered them into plastic garbage bags
tied them tightly
suffocating the deceased.

Only then would I marvel at life, green and small, burrowing out.

It's early in the season
only a little dirt under my fingernails, a little sunburn.

It's early when I enter sagging
the morning shower and shave winter from ivory legs, emerge
Botticellian, a young nymph.
Not enough green yet to brainwash me
make me forget how clean and soft my feet were
fingernails clear
in the dead of winter.
How heartbroken and mad
I had been all throughout
believing myself
pure and clean and cool.

One Night

This almost despair—
it's possible to wake up feeling.
Where does it come from?
I haven't the courage to say how lonely
I am at certain times.
don't want to frighten anyone with my shroud
of loneliness
that's how considerate I am.

Oh, one is bound to regress.
I am bound.
As I confront who I am not
pretending just a little to be other than I am
on the way to who I must be.

I need to find one night
that I can live all the way through.
I'm going to fall backward
into splendor
bequeathing myself to myself.

I have a taste for despair
but it's a fleeting taste
I can never sustain.

After, I feel lazy.
Think about watching old movies until they blur
become forgotten dreams
that I half-believe were past lives.
I feel lazy and imagine folding
poems small, tying them with utmost resistance
discreet, tucking them into the secret world
I always hoped they would reach
affixing them behind cracked, smudged mirrors
under beds that creak
and in the rear of cluttered closets.

I'm lazy but no longer lonely.
You could say I have the consideration
most days to pin my happiness
on all the many words hidden in the interstices
of an empty room in disrepair.
You could say I have the consideration
one night a year to feel the feverish equilibrium
of being awake, so late.

Invisible, Unfinished

And then, on the path.
The one on which I prided myself
on having noticed all the variations of ferns
and the hue of Saskatoon berries
the narrow blue glimpses of hidden flowers.
It was on the path of deepest magic
where I first encountered the sound of the soul
being swallowed
and the soul
was almost unmistakably mine.

It is a grave accident of moments
when the animal leaps out.
Time collapses
and I'm standing, I stand before it, atremble.
The worst is that I already feel the humiliation
that should come after
cold sweat of an utter devastation.
I am like a forgotten flower pressed into a thick book
taken outside and opened under the sun
to choke on the petalled dust of myself.

Exactly now I must choose
whether to lie down or to run
though the only choice is to be eaten, digested.
I might refuse anything but the tender grinding
invisible, unfinished
the meat and bones and hair of me.

Later, clothed now, as I am
with this garment of the deep, of devourment
traveling, mingling, in the chamber
of the animal's stomach
this is how you will know me
or fail to know me
the cost of the passage.
As for me, I've yet to call out the correct name
or to ascertain how to carve bone into knife
how to make that one quick incision
to make good my escape.

You ask, is it fierce?
I believe the devourer to be a meek dignitary, but one that is a master at finding pain spots.

Alone, Alone, Alone, Together

Are you one of those people who think it's enough
to say the word just once?

I'm not fool enough to write that I lose patience
with the brutal solitude of motherhood.
I'm not the fool to write
alone three times
and leave it at that.

Have you heard the one about the novelist's grim story
of dying children
coming true years after?

Even poets have to be careful.
Not to write about hunger too diligently
or about being adrift
without thinking of a future better spent on shore.
We must take care with our metaphors.
And neither write overmuch on effort, nor on ease.

Would you set in ink
flowered descriptions of lit candles by drapery
or telegrams, unread, on a table by the open window?

When I yearn for the calm solitude of this room—
away from the pretty summer horde, screaming, damp
that fever pitch of always wanting more of something, small things, as
we all do—
let it be heard, I meant temporarily
sequestered, intact.

All week I've been trying to remember who said
that whoever remembers childhood best, wins.
I've forgotten who and I'm doing my best to forget my future.
But the book of my childhood
I knew at last I could write it
when I read the lines in the procession of wet footprints, sand and grass
and a few sane tears on my freshly washed kitchen floor.

It Makes Sense

The background to this story I don't want to tell
and maybe I shouldn't
has to do with the orange kitten someone gave me
when I lived in the tall and falling down house
its brick foundation rippling and held in place
by bunches of car jacks.
The kitten is the background because she disappeared
and after wandering the neighborhood for days calling
I had the idea to open the closed door
to the room under renovation by the landlord
the room with walls full of newspapers.
And the brick that was supposed to be holding
up the window had turned into my cat.

A lifetime later
I live in a solid house with a lawn that I water too much.
My daughter's cat
whom I have long dismissively suspected
is the reincarnation of my brother
disappeared one night.
I don't believe in reincarnation of course
but it makes sense
my brother comes back as a cat
so I can at last love
or admit to loving him
then he disappears to traumatize my daughter
gets hit by a car or just disappears
just disappears.
A runaway. It would be just like him.

But the cat was there all along, hiding in a pile of clothes.
When we'd given up searching
there was the cat
dreamy and stretching
walking down the stairs
laughing at me.
It makes sense after all that we see the dead in the living
keep acting out tired old scenes
frayed at the edges
those of us who cannot live in despair
those of us who cannot make sense of the hints the universe
relentlessly throws our way.
Instead we resort to flinging the front door open
calling and calling with all our feeble might.

Curlicues

After three days of rain I enter
the morning on a glittering emerald carpet
the backyard dense with talk and murmuring.
I picked a flower like that woman in a Roman fresco
who nips it as though she's holding a bone china teacup
as though she's just heard a story, or maybe just another piece
a new bit of a story she's heard before.
Whatever it is
she's gripped the ridiculously tiny handle until it snaps.

When I pick the flower
there's shattering, spillage, the swishing and swirling of skirts.

Next I go on to pluck the browning heads of marigolds
then come to drink my diet coke
another of my true addictions
and maybe the neighbors whose huge windows
blink at me incredulous and accusing
are behind them shaking their heads.

They don't know they have before them a woman
from the 2nd century B.C.
In their condescension, they don't understand that the scent of marigold
from my yellowed fingertips gathers around my pen
and turns these lines into strands of golden hair
which might belong to a woman gripping a teacup
or plucking a flower painted quick deft and loose.

Which reminds me, last night I dreamed of trying to ride
an impossibly tall horse bareback.
All night I was half falling off
but somehow managing to stay on
because I was holding these long braided reins
of marigold hair beaded with lapis lazuli.
I was as a kite on the end of these reins
flying up and then landing on the chestnut back of this leggy creature.

Yesterday I read an essay that spoke with distaste
of decorative poetry and while I read
I wholeheartedly agreed.
But this morning bathed in the sun's bequest
drinking sweet nothings
I can say naught against decorating pages and reams
with strands of gold, dreams, windows, frescoes and flowers
for the news from the past travels most furtively
and sometimes in the rough form of curlicues and visible gestures
that we must hold like beautiful reins seemingly attached
only to dream horses.

I'm Tired of Being Summoned

That much of existence is quivering and tangled.
That we hardly feel the depths of ourselves
through skin to marrow.
The beauty of our own existence seldom rises
up and out of us
but mostly remains as an unlit light
or an Aladdin's lamp, un-rubbed.

I've been earnest in my attempts to answer the summons
to swim toward the lamp which must rest in a daydream sea.
Constantly pulled off course
by the end of the day I'm just grateful
to have made it to the shore, licked
covered in sand.

I once held the belief
(you see I once held beliefs)
that the surest way in was away.
I have always listened in horror and shock
to stories of people who have never left
their own village or enclave.
I have been filled with pity for their lack of wanderlust
for whatever must have gone wrong or fallen through
to have taken away their urge to go farther than the grocery store.

And maybe I'll never board a plane and fly from here again.
It's implausible anyway, flying.
So is swimming.
It's implausible that our bodies could be held so
by either water or aircraft.
I readily accede to the unbearable weight of myself.

I'm tired of being summoned and failing to answer.
I want to be the old woman hefting delicate-ripe tomatoes
in her rickety bird-claw hand at the market
traveling the inward seas and skies
answering only to that inner light
which she has never had to tell her legs and arms to strive for
because she has that otherworldly confidence
that the lamp is not the clumsy product of tangled up poetic devices
but rather easily contained
such as the light within the tomato is held by an impossibly thin skin.

It's no wonder I'm so tired
inventing old women, their paper sacks full of tomatoes
and over-earnestly calculating the distance to the nearest market.
I've been afraid to answer my summons with the simple question
how do I get to the divine?

This Time

This time I am repelled. But I eat my lunch in front of it all the same.
Just now it has deftly scurried across the huge web it has spun between
the house and the railing of the gray deck. It's under the railing, hiding
from me, or is it the wind. It's me. It has read my murderous thoughts.
Unlike G.H. I could never consume this—the largest spider I have ever
seen in the wild. My cheese sandwich is thick in my throat.

Does it think I missed seeing its other incarnations?

Does it think I didn't recognize the web it strung earlier this summer
above my daughter's green plastic lawn chair
from the other side of the railing to the pink flowering shrub?
Does it think I don't understand
that climbing the stairs will now feel like running the gauntlet to me?

And now it hides from me.
I suppose it knows I never place my hand on the railing when I ascend.
I suppose it knows my passion for watering.
That it was I who at last, after many weeks of noting
that unspidered web
accumulating its sun-dried suckled out victims,
it was I who struck out at it with the long watering wand
and destroyed it.

It knows too that I have just this moment realized
that the web I leaned into
last week with my face
the web that smeared and stuck to my eyeglasses, blinding me
belonged also to it.

This spider knows I feel it creeping in my hair
though I believe it yet to be under the railing.
The spider knows I am a coward, at last, but yes
a passionate coward with a yearning for a cheap victory, a deluge.
Already
I begin to tremble.

Solitude and Return

How to return.
It may well be a question, life's question
of how to come back.
Not pure enough to rise.
How could I believe I'm pure enough to rise?

For I've ended friendships over an un-returned book.
For I've stolen horses at night, cutting them from the herd, sharp.

It's settled that I, too, will be returning.
I speak of this out of the grandeur of an authority—
the authority of a newly gained confidence in a personal earthly paradise.
Where are we if we can't accept magic, however decayed?

Solitude is the way.

It's true—that you can find a solitude once
and carry it with you into the unknown, toward the breaches.
Several times I've invented my own solitude, that magic
even lately with the hum of cars from the highway
and the din of the suburbs.
I file them, my loveliest solitudes
into an accordion folder such as accountants use.
My capacity to imagine solitudes is such
that even my future solitudes are insistent and resplendent.
When I return
once as a lost book, a thousand years of dust
and once as a horse, a thousand years more of dust
I'll file the dust in there too and see how that plays.

I'll return and return
to accumulate the silt and decayed magic of the pure.
Solitude upon solitude will collect
in my jubilant subconscious.

Even so, I can't help but feel compassion for myself
since I believe that the excellent oblivion is revealed
slow and bright, with a charming patience
and I was unceremoniously thrown out of charm school
and long ago gave up on trying to be patient.
I should have been trying to answer the question
how to rise, how to become pure enough to rise?
That's always been my folly—
to be seduced into answering the wrong questions
because they possessed a measure of elegance.

Feeding the Path

The birds will exact the breadcrumbs.
There one goes in the gullet of a sparrow.
It flies so high and drops
back to earth lost without disgrace.

When laying out the bright stones that will take one home
who ever thinks of the little drab birds?
Too heavy and unreckless to rise
starving into the blue forest.

A Frail Clarity

I scrape and learn nothing.
I am awash aswim adrift. Dumb as water.
But then, a frail clarity.
At last I understand the secret I planted in my garden
and which is my destiny.

Last night was my hundredth dream of becoming a hermit.
Even hermits know inundation, notate the variations of solitude,
the visitations of songbirds to an upheld and empty palm.
Know that our destinies reside in the fawn pouch of childhood
we wear on a chafing string around our necks.

Yes, the secret of my garden is the absence
of a ring of birch trees
and that my destiny is that ring of birch trees.

But is the absence of the trees my destiny
or the trees themselves
or is it to collect the filmy, flimsy leavings
and press them to my lips
before placing them in the flame
in the flame of that candle which must reside precisely
in the center
of the circle
of trees
amid the small and fierce tangle of the forest floor?
Or is my destiny to return to the flame, dumb as water
to preserve the gray, white and black of the trees
which surely would
ignite.
If not, then why have I always known
that the pouch around my neck is filled with
ashes?

Called Away

I was called away
from that sunrise
and it came to nag at me.
I never made it back to the window over the kitchen sink
I never made it back to polish the faucet
or to look again at the sunrise.
It was getting dark before it came to me again
while I drained the pasta and the steam filled the window.
I could have looked out another window then, witnessed the sun setting.
But it had already started and I craved something whole.

After that, I wanted to write down in my diary the colours
at least the colours, and the way they were stretched
in their easy ravishing glory
so thin.
Just that.
Each time I was called away.
It didn't want me, this sunrise,
and I gave it up, clear.

Instead I sat in my red velvet chair
wanting everything.
It was only a minute, maybe two.
I wore over my eyes the cruel veils
and I became at long last—
even amid the interruptions—red velvet.
I'd forgotten so much, gone slack.
And then,
had I wanted
I couldn't even come clean on all my pseudonyms
they were gone, gone
and in their place, strange placenta
a red velvet smoking jacket, red velvet trousers
I felt myself to be one, solemnly invisible.

Thin-Skinned

I won't lie, I began.
For a long while I worked on the jeweled scales.
I studied the epidermises of crocodiles, salamanders
in particular salamanders.
Once I even almost entered the flames.
Not yet thick enough.
I carried on.

Now I find it difficult, awkwardly personal
to describe how it came to be
that I welded steel and quaver set stones naked.
I made headway. If I'd continued
I'd be speaking to you now from out of the flames.

But why not make it a point to consider advice
to the contrary?
I only had to ask myself what precisely it mattered
whether beneath thick or thin
that the humiliation would be draped?

My skin becomes taut
you can almost see through it held up so to the sun
though the scraping goes on.
The scars, luckily, for the most part, are off to the edges
so it only remains to be seen
whether my reinvention will be in folio, quarto, or octavo.

Why Not

We're not going anywhere exotic
we're staying put.
I keep making sincere and ludicrous pacts with myself
eat more fruits and vegetables
exercise more, forget more
forget to look in the mirror and forget to watch the news.
I've made a pact with myself to live in this house forever
and I'm staying in the suburbs, I'm staying put.

Last week we bought a cement statue
of an unknown Roman lady looking over her right shoulder
and we struggled her up into the niche made for a television.
We're weighing down the place two hundred pounds at a time.
The news around here is ancient, heavy.

Since she arrived I've been taking my glass of wine
at the kitchen table as I've always done
that one glass of heaven before dinner
accompanied.
Now, after one of those long and beautiful days
the beauty mostly lost in the bustle and fatigue
when I ask, why do I ever complain?
I receive a sidelong glance
at my brief drunkenness
the flowers on the table
at the verdigris of this wild bliss
this small, rough, inelegant life.

Doesn't every moment contain a secret truth?
If only it could be taken inward
and that one could follow spiraling into the fire of oneself.

This morning alone I sat outside
in the new green of spring
remembering every other spring I greeted with disbelief.
All winter I dreamed of Hawaii
who can blame me?
but if I made it there I wouldn't believe it either.
Maybe I'd spend all my time climbing to the mouths of volcanoes
so I could express my incredulity to the utmost.

I have a terrible memory but sometimes a line will get into my
thoughts
and repeat over and over.
Today the words from the desert fathers,
why not be totally changed into fire?
I'm not going anywhere.
I've made a pact with a sidelong glance, with disbelief
I've made a pact with the question.
Why not be?

I've Let Myself Go

I drop my daughter off at school
and when I get home I leave again
to go walking on the gravel path at the edge
of the suburbs too close to the highway.
My hamstrings pull and ache
I've let myself go
my breathing hard
other things too.
My hair is the same style it was ten years ago
but it's dry now, so very dry.
When did I stop wearing mascara?
(It hurt my eyes and obstructed my vision).
When did I stop buying my clothes a size too small?
When did I let myself go?

I let myself go.
I walk on the path at the edge
wear comfortable sandals and even though it's warm
conceal my knees with capri pants instead of wearing shorts.
I stop by the stand of trees that once belonged to a farmyard
and notice the saplings, the long row of them, that seem
to have flung themselves from out of that old thicket.
And they have, they have.

I'm going down the path
my heart beats faster and faster.
And my blood is thickening
maybe it's turning black like mascara
I'll let it change into ink.
If I look to the side I can see the cars across the field
whizzing by me
all the while
I imagine my skin is metamorphosing into bleached paper
it's wishful thinking
but I'm flinging myself down the path
at least the sap of me is that much further ahead
I'm letting myself go.

Blue Girl

In the garden, behind the new trellis
built to hide us from eyes in the tall houses
I find I'm tired of myself.
I've been wanting sincere annunciations
to pierce screaming
golden into my dispirit.
The thing is I'm happy but it's aflutter
tinged by an uncontrolled blue.
I'm angry at the reticence of my happiness.

I've been pretending it's possible to be
a hermit, fervent in the suburbs
I'm pretending there's such a thing
and that I've been there
only need to get back to trembling
aloof and wild and ringing with fear
just as it was last summer.

I think this and then
the clouds come in, rolling, ambling
and I have to go indoors or be swallowed cold
obliterated by their daydream silence.
What was last summer anyway
but a repetition of what will be this one?

Away from the eyes
I'm back to drawing self-portraits.
Do you know how many drawing pads I filled this past winter?
I make up the rules for myself—don't lift the pen
draw holding breath
be fluid, fluid, fluid
exhalation means stop.
Scribbles, they're all scribbles, each one.
But I started off using black ink, then switched to sepia
and now, suddenly, the scribbles clamor for ink
blue as ashes or stained glass.

Every time the drawing ends, the breathing resumes
I'm stabbed, the message, a pinprick treading water in the unraveling.
I go for weeks hungry for a sign that there's a life in me
my life, the spark of myself.
I still can't see the radiance that I've been foolishly waiting for.
I flip through pages and pages of drawings, looking for the end points
but they've healed without even leaving bruises.

I remember years ago standing in front of the gates
of the Peggy Guggenheim Museum
the coloured glass hurled at and tangled in the metal web.
Me wanting to cry
or maybe it's only now that I want to cry.
Because I wish I'd stood there longer.
Because I hadn't then read the message of the broken
polished glass eyes.
The way they were caught, held, stopped
then I must have thought was tragic.
I didn't even notice how the light must enter
changed.

In my hiddenness I hadn't understood
the message of the threshold
the annunciation according to C.L.—
each of us is responsible for the entire world.
I begin to see that it arrives and arrives
out of and into the blue
at least a thousand times a day.

Subterraneous Re-enchantment

In the spring we, overeager, lure friends into our backyard gardens
saying, here, these shoots will be peonies
and over here there will be marvelous poppies.
We tell of remarkable flowers, yellow giants
and of vines, excessively fragrant
from our mouths a palette of fugitive colours spills.
We are the tour guides to what will be, to the unreachable
and to our own subterraneous re-enchantment.

Now, midsummer.
And friends are busy
tending their own gardens, frantically refusing to imagine
as we are, the end of paradise.
We resort to taking photographs
proof of an unearthly beauty, unexpected portals.
But the wondrous is transfigured, incommensurate.
The sky, the joy, the heat, all missing.
The way the big clouds like ships
cruise above us and cast true and mysterious shadows
on all that we say and all that we don't say.

Someone arrives and we try to stir up just a little envy
because even we are incomprehensibly envious of all this glory.
We talk breezily now in the thick hum of bees.
This is when we walk on the perfect grass and speak, lacking decorum
of what was
in front of all that is.
The poppies have bloomed and gone.
How fine the irises were.
We might as well be relating dreams.
No one really listens to dreams recounted.

At the end of summer we shall divorce ourselves
from whatever manages to unfurl into the last minutes
after we have been self-expelled, soul-wintered.
The stonecrop is valiant then, yet entirely remote.
All we see is snow.
Here is where we curse, slightly, the imagination
that has us seeing again, what submersions the future must hold.
An imagination that colludes with the ripeness of our delimitations.

At the end of summer, after the finality, we are funeral directors
with no choice but to leave the casket to the substratum open.
Don't look, we want to yell, avert your eyes.
But no one ever does. No one ever can.

Salt

I'm the sort of person who flirts with sadness.
It's a dangerous hobby but so far
when I drink of emptiness
the next cup overflows.

When we sat on the vast cement patio
overlooking the sea more than a decade ago
I didn't then understand how the past
floats into the present just like ships coming into port
all day long and even into the night.
We were waiting all afternoon in Civitavecchia, the old city
for the night ferry to Sardegna.
We didn't know that our tiny cabin
would be a closet by the engine room
or that we wouldn't dream that night.

That afternoon we sipped sparkling lemonade
and wrote postcards home
under huge umbrellas and we drank up the sea.
I'd only read about the sea and it was pure
gentle magic, and madness too.
I was beyond happy then so that in all the photographs
my eyes are glistening
but you can't make out the diamonds at the corners of my eyes.

Now whenever I'm sitting outside writing letters or in my diary
I think of that afternoon
it's there with me, here it is.
But also mingled with these thoughts
the poem by Amichai, dog-eared in my copy
where he writes a letter on a hotel balcony
a tear falls and he circles it.

To whom did we write those postcards?
What pictures did we send?
Why didn't I write a long letter to myself?
Because now I want details, I want the silt of all that afternoon.
I can't even picture the boats off in the distance
or the birds that must have flown above us.
I can't remember my lost dreams
and I want to compare them to the ones that slip away from me now
and the ones that don't.
I can't remember the scent of the air, the way it touched my cheek
more gently than the soul breaks, if it were to break.

Why didn't I send myself a postcard drawn over with a flurry of circles
in invisible ink?
Because no one sends tears of happiness, nor did they in past centuries.
They'd only be misconstrued and anyway
I've no real need for circles with arrows drawn
what I want is the salt, gathered into a saucer
so I can rim each glass
the full ones, the empty ones.
I want to taste the salt of each.
But it's useless to attempt becoming a connoisseur of salt
you can't separate the salt of happiness from the salt of sadness.
Salt isn't like a wine
with a complicated bouquet, a surprising finish.

Postcards all say one thing—dream.
And salt,
salt says—thirst.

A Black Horse Running After

- After reading the Diary of Etty Hillesum before bed

At the last minute I remember
the recurring dream of the racing black train.
The deafening noise of the steam
the darkness thick, so very thick
and still the coal black train could exist within it
and I
had one hope to erase myself from the scene
which had something to do
but not entirely
with retrieving my collection of pennies
and proving it was indeed a substantial collection.
There were things going on in the train
that I knew I couldn't know about
only I knew that if I didn't escape—
death.
And I knew that no one else could jump
it was going too fast
and they would all—

I awoke
each time, soaking wet, shivering
in another room
for quite some time before having the thought
to cry out.
And then my father came and kissed my forehead and put me back
from whence I had come
and asked me what the nightmare had been
and I said a black train in the black night
which wasn't it at all.

Three times I had this dream as a child
once as an adult.

Last night's dream began with
I jumped from a train in the dark and then
began the ordeal of hiding.
Running all through the night
until daylight
being buried in a hollowed out hill
in the cave wall.
The dirt, gray, chalk-like
and a straw to breathe from
thin screaming breaths.
Knowing it wouldn't work.

*

What does the dream want?
Does the one dream finish, at last, the other?
What dream will finish the second?
What had I been reading before bed thirty years ago?
(I'd never thought to ask this though the dream
has made a dark well in me for thirty years or more).
Can a life enter another life through dreams?
And the black horse, where was she?
You see there is a vague memory
so vague it is hardly that
I seem to remember a black horse running after the train.
Yes, I'm sure there was
a black horse running after.

Leaving the Room

That I knew enough to mourn in the beforehand
this is my slim consolation.

You can never take up from where you left off.

I've been back for days now
folding the thin edge of myself over and again.
I've taken an inventory of pollen
the dry-damp souls that left acute traces on my soul
like lily pollen on a best linen shirt.
You can't brush the pollen away
the only course being inward, to let it drop down
one excruciating molecule at a time.

I was away
called, even.
When I came back
nothing about the room was the same.
It's as though someone came in the night and moved
the furniture a millimeter in one direction or another.
And the box which held the dreamed of secret complexity
has been tied in rough twine and too well knotted.

Remembering is a contortion.
All that I have been is poured
into the squeeze of these new early mornings
and I find I don't know what I wanted
to know.
I'm a desperate amnesiac in love and in hate with the blankness.
Still I want to make something beautiful
out of all these desperate breaths and this ink flow
(it's only the ink that remembers me, and I it)
and the long drinks from the trough
of the blue window, slightly askew.
I'm trying half-hearted
to stop the flow to stop asking the questions.

When will I cross over?
When will the pollen sink into the red velvet forest?

Lost

Reversal

I am always—starting over, lost.
First it was insomnia
and now the robin is singing
so that I lose my spot
and just as the blithe flowers are preparing themselves
like Olympic athletes
for the sadness of a peak performance.

I won't say why the insomnia
for the same reason I won't question the robin.
I would rather talk of the weather.

Oh it's true I lack
many skills.
Sometimes I lose sleep over them.
But I will not yearn to become a proficient
at party talk.
I want to grip souls
with the sharp edges of mine
measure each.

I do prefer to talk of the weather.
There's real heart in that, drama, desire.
What did you see in the clouds today?
What child are you?
And oh, the unspeakable depths of a thick morning fog…

This very moment the clouds are rough sketches
of themselves
lining up to pay homage to the sun
casting huge shadows on me, intermittent.

One minute, I'm drenched in the tone of goddesses
the next I'm holding my papers to the underworld.
My submission to each is equal.

As it was the night of my rare insomnia.
Though I knew myself to be forsaken
and I knew myself faithless.
yet I did find recompense
in the way the moon and the streetlight combined
to throw weak light, plainly miraculous
through the living room window
onto the painting of pomegranates, my pomegranates
as I wandered without sound
my life in a reversal
much like a painting seen in a mirror
or the mirrors that are in paintings, reflecting a side of things
that otherwise wouldn't have been imagined.

Apparition of the Clearing

I want
the apparition of the clearing
its lion company.
I do not forget.

The forest holds me and
I love the forest.
I love its half-trails and mosses
the chewed bits and the texture of its barks
its berried brambles, and the way it hides
bluebells and tiger-lilies, tremulously
in the low spots, in the bright.
I love the green embrace, each step
into the uncertain labyrinth.
The great trees,
they hold me.
The frail green undergrowth
which nonetheless springs up
after being trodden on,
the spider webs
broken on my cheeks,
for these I am full of pity and remorse.

But it's the song of the clearing
top gone
insane soaring
that occurs in the carefully imprecise
treasury of the forest.

I lose my way there if I can.
If it will allow.

I seem to live for those moments
when it is clear from earth to heaven
when it is clear they are one.
They meet each other, mingle
bodies in pure ravishment.
The emerald floor of the forest
the sapphire sky—
who can say which is which?

Talisman

It's not enough to collect examples of poems lost and almost lost.
It's not enough to tell the stories.
Soyinka's prison poems, *The Man Died*
written in perilous secret between the lines of another book.
Dickinson's poems folded and tied in twine
hidden in boxes and drawers.
Fernando Pessoa's trunk filled with scrap notes
for *The Book of Disquiet.*

It's not enough to tell about the spiritual notebook
Rumi carried with him, written by his father
and which Shams of Tabriz drowned in the fountain.

Byron loved telling the story of how pages
of Richardson's *Pamela* were used to wrap bacon.
He wrote that his own cantos might be used to line portmanteaus.

It's not enough to imagine other uses for poetry.
It's not enough to imagine sending paper boats floating down the
river
or burying sheaves of paper at the foot of the apple tree.
It's better to get on with the cherished unlivable ceremonies
the drowning and burning, the folding, knotting and burial.

Come with me
I'll show you how I shred poems
how I dig in the dirt with bare hands
I'll show how much lighter fluid to pour onto a glossy cover
and how far back to stand.
Dirt has seeped into pores
the pads of my fingers are numb from reaching into flame
turning the pages so that each page receives.
The sides of my hands are chafed from the rough twine
I've used to tie up the remains.
There is no end to this work.

Let me put all this another way.
These ceremonies of water, ashes, dirt and twine are part of the art form.
These are ceremonies of polite radiance.
In thrall to the music of ruins I'm learning at last how to write bedazzled
into the flames into failure, loss.
Learning all this and how to keep it a shattering phantom secret.

Assassination Plot

The wrong word comes out.
This is fine.
I'm among friends who know the red map
that appears on my face.
I believe they can read it and know
where I had really meant to take them.

Sometimes a whole row of words leaves me
and I know, just a moment too late
that they're not quite right.
There they go, shiny regiment in mismatched uniforms
marching into the fray
a humiliating battle.
They're about to be massacred
but they can't turn back.
They lie down and try to disappear
mix their indecipherable blood with the loam.

I'm saved by words that are handwritten.
I sit in my room and write silent letters to myself
letters full of the wounded.
A redolence of damp earth and thyme about them.

Only now and then a shimmering string
knotted and teased into cat's cradle.

How to write them down with my fingers so imprisoned?

Doing Other

For such a long while
I thought I would learn to paint.
Fixed a point in the future to become devoted
occasionally mixed up colours
and attacked a canvas with a self-portrait.
There was the mangled Doge, though I meant him no harm.
A copy or two of a Dufy and doubly tormented Picassos.
I think I would have been happy to be mediocre.

Embroidery always appealed to the mortally wounded side of me.
The spooled thread in shops arrayed by colour and hue
are alone wonderful to contemplate.
The thought was pleasing—
making tiny stitches on starched linen pillow cases—
dream outlines—blue horses, honeysuckle vines,
cabbage roses, the tree of life.

There was a time when I imagined I would ride a horse all day
in the wind, fast.
Or that I would live and walk endlessly in the forest.

I would have been happy growing flowers or keeping bees.
I would have been happy surrounded by whatever sweetness.

I could have been a cloud watcher.
The ones this morning are particularly fine
moving at a delightful pace, as dreams do
in nights at the sweltering fringes of summer.

I would have liked devoting myself to a diary, just that.
Each volume tightly bound in silk or brocade.
With each one, a new life, clear.
One dark, one simple and wild, one intricate and
secretly devastating.
One filled with the late afternoon light from an open window.
Such a delicate and close script I would have developed, too.
The ink trails an enticing undergrowth.

And yet, and yet, I have been drawn
into this muddy pool of love
and will drown here in this mad happiness
undistracted.

The Rain is Unromantic

This began like a personal ad.
I poured myself a cup of coffee
and raised myself up to knock against

the lesser angels with their besmirched robes
I looked out the rear window, clean
and was joyous—
all that is green was greener.

I'm the sort content to look out windows
at the falling and drink coffee angelically
the word rain firm in the cave of my mouth.

I look out the front window and begin to worry.
For all the trees that bend and bend.
The new one we planted—its stake has given way.
Every fiber of it clings
gloriously, hellishly
to what?
Somewhere, it comprehends, a tree is snapping in half.
I ignore it.
I squint out at a thousand years of rain
the tedium of it leading me to pace.

The rain is not romantic.
It brings this wind to threaten my gangly lilac tree
whose blooms have just withered.
Why would it bring the wind?

I go into the elements with a hammer
some string, another stake.
The rain assaults my glasses
I move small rocks and claw until I reach earth
and then I pound and pound.

I wait now, dampened, with spots on my glasses
mud under my fingernails
wrists throbbing.
I am ready for the rain and its murderous compatriots.
Uncomprehending, I'm the sort content
to look out windows at rain, besmirched, unvanquished.

Falling Short

It's too true that by now I'm off-balance
losing my nerve for one thing and another.
I'm unnerved by the sheer number of dragonflies this summer
their bodies an astonishing variety of colours
their wings, incomprehensibly transparent.
I've lost my nerve to reach out and touch what is delicate
and fitful in its response to the immensity
of all that is not to be alighted upon
but rather flown through, undiscerned.

Baudelaire said that anything that falls short
of the sublime is reprehensible
and I know it to be true.
And I sorrow before the requisite temptation to believe otherwise.

When you lose your nerve for one thing
I tell you, there is a cascade, a complete degradation.
I sorrow in my backyard, tallying up
all the things I've lost my nerve for.
Driving, cooking, sleep.
All the same, I do these things, my fear
unleashing an imperceptible shivering in my chest.
You'd never know with what temerity I shake dried spices into a sauce
or with what tangled courage it takes
to breathe deliberately, to lie in bed with every appearance
of having benign dreams.

I came outside to calm myself and instead began to register
everything that wasn't calming.
One neighbor shovels gravel
and another picks imminent green apples from boughs
in danger of breaking.
The loathsome noise of all that weight being lifted.
Further off, a basketball hits the pavement unto eternity.
The clattering sounds of breakfast, hungers sated.
A car starts, travels away.

Bees hum, wind shatters the quiet of leaves
somewhere a fountain trickles, a fly buzzes
a grasshopper clicks into the air in a fearsome trajectory
a door opens, a phone rings
the wind rattles once again in the dogwoods
a ghost butterfly brushes my shoulder, burning.
I throw the remainder of my cold coffee onto the grass and return indoors.

I sorrow before requisite temptations
I careen through the noise of the world, fitful and fearful
struck with awe at all that falls short of the sublime
and all that doesn't.

But the Gods are Organized

I'm at peace again.
This is so frequent that it doesn't bear
remarking upon.
I am too congenial
not with the unreachable axe but instead
with the frozen heart
its clear dissolve into blood wine.

I've dreamt of fame—who hasn't?
But such dreams for me fall
into ruins as quickly as a Hollywood set
all thanks to my hedonism and slow reflexes.

The gods of the hoop and stick, the wheel of life
accepted my bribe and there has to be a cost.
Part of which is being strung out in all directions
in sepia like Leonardo's drawing of the universal man.

Why have the gods let me get away with all these irregular spokes
the long painless stretches?
I imagine they idly spin me toward a slope, a precipice
Awake at night I listen to the claps of thunder
counting backwards.
Thinking of ways to outwit the gods
to steer them from anguish.
I try not to worry about the fate of those who've been caught
the fury the gods then unleash.
I try not to worry about lightning strikes.

I've struck so many deals with the gods it's difficult to keep them straight.
But the gods are organized.
There's no point in believing otherwise.
They giddily mete out payment and punishment
until I'm vertiginous.

They let me drink my cheap blood wine and I pretend
to be dizzy and clumsy
so they don't know I do notice
out of the corner of my bleary eye
that the stick that spins this sparking wheel of life
is, in actual fact, the axe.

Lost

Company last night.
So that the morning is filled with
thoughts of others' lives
and with sweeping up crumbs
and collecting crumpled flowery napkins
which were dabbed at between
Spanish wine and Roquefort cheese
cake and coffee, calm revelations from the depths.

We spoke of the sensation
being out of step
which is what happens when you constantly examine
the flow of your existence
backward and forward and backward to now.
I remember I tried to describe the lost feeling
I have when my daughter is not with me
how I go about doing errands
and it's me that's lost, not her.

We talked about friends we no longer have
books on the shelf
assiduously gathering dust
books the eye deliberately jumps over.

The evolution of the self.
All of the conditions placed on the spirit.
The things we thought we knew and instead
keep returning to with changed hearts.
We talked about these.

Arranging things before our guests arrived
my daughter kissed one wineglass, for me
so that I would remember her while she slept
the dull noise of adult voices like a cat's paw under her door.
And I did remember her all through
forgetting her though, too, all the while.

This morning my head aches a little from the wine
and maybe from those aching moments
when someone lets you hold some of their life
in the rough-hewn cradle of your own.
How fine and rare that is.
That we can, however briefly,
enter into each others' difficult understanding.

Last night, I touched lips to a glass for remembrance
and the next day fill the sink with scalding water and sunlight.
It's that fleeting then, that easily washed away, our meetings.
And yet I doubt them not
and wander lost but without despair.

The Extremities of an Innocence

What's left to be done?
The cat drinks from the bird bath
and I sit in the cool fall air, falling.
Forward.

The dogwoods need shaping, training
so they arch one into the other, embrace.
The cat looks through the fence slats to the neighbor's yard.
Poised there for an eternity.
I envy the concentration.
I've a sapling yet to plant.
There are all the flower petals I meant to dry.

The cat walks on air through the monkshood.
I need to pick the apples, soon, soon.
They've grown only on the sunny side of the tree
so from where I sit
it looks barren.

The cat examines the columbine
sniffs the coneflowers, the phlox.
I might need to learn to live like a cat free in the labyrinth
though I fear it's too late.
I need to find the extremities of an innocence
and live there.

How does one find the secret mirrors hidden in one's backyard
let alone in one's own life?

This past week I learned that I need to be more kindly.
Softer.
I'm not even sure quite how I learned that
or quite how to become so.

This week my daughter was insistent she needed
a diary with a lock and key.
I didn't know that she knew such things existed
only five years old.
What would she put in it, I asked.
Secrets. Pictures and letters.
So it begins.

It seems we are born full of secrets
and maybe it is at five that we have the correct sense of that.

I write things in my diary like—
I don't know whether to starve myself
or feed myself in the early mornings.
I don't know how to come clean.

And I don't, I truly do not.

I've done my fair share of skulking.
I too have taken long glimpses through the slats
at others' lives.

Everywhere I look there's something to be done
but mostly I just sit.
Even the cat will drink from the bath of the bird she would eat.
I can hardly swallow
what's in my throat.

There's so much to be done.
What was the object of this garden?
I can't remember the green messages I had meant to send myself.

I only know that my daughter's diary came with two keys.
We tied a ribbon to each and one she gave to me.
I have come to understand
there is the key that opens and the one
that refrains.

Reminder

And I had forgotten that disastrous need to look back.
To stop and fully turn around and stand, and look, agape.
Knowing even a slender glance over the shoulder
would precipitate this.
I had forgotten the need to tell myself repeatedly—
feet forward eyes forward.
So what if you'd fail psychoanalysis.
Work on the peripheral vision
work on the mind's eye.
Everything behind you is in front too—
mirrors will abound.

Blundering Reconciliations

How to live well? How to reach the inner hum, the harmony?
Without guilt.
But mother guilt never dissolves. It's a concession.
I know this from when I thought there could be no child –
that being without would be, for me, intolerable.
Then, I knew the sensation the sleeping wolf learned.
The wolf who had swallowed the kid goats whole
but woke up with rocks sewn instead into his belly.

I have traded rocks for guilt, happily.

All these blundering reconciliations
of dreams and desires and home and family and self.

I know the potency of dreams.
I've walked into them, I've made a point of dreaming toward dreams.
But this morning I'm tired and it seems false, futile.
Pulled in every direction, tired, awake, it's difficult to dream.
Sometimes at the end of the dream, there's merely exasperation.
Tomorrow, I'll do what I can.

All Manner of Things

- for Lee and for Barb

And my fate and my sorrow are holding quiet meetings
of the most secretive nature in a dark corner of my soul.

But it's not as simple as that.
Other forces are at work.

In one week, three occasions.
Two of the best people I have known
send me the words of Julian of Norwich.
All shall be well, and all shall be well, and all manner of things shall be well.

Then, I pick up a book, the third.

Today, a pristine headache.
Walking through the air like razors, that cold.
The ache so bad I thought I would fall to my knees
on the sparsely sanded ice.
I did make it to the car and sat for a while
in a state of refusal.
I know not what I was refusing and still go on refusing.
I drank a box of chocolate milk
then I drove carefully, carefully.
All the hurtling distant lives so close to mine.

On the freeway, it arrived.
The snow and the words, or the words and the snow.
And my head—smoothed.
The huge flakes like messages
no two alike.
An exchange occurred.
What for what?
I don't want to ask, I don't want to answer.
Another refusal, soft and bright.

Possible Gods

-I wrote these poems while thinking, in these penultimate steps of my life, I repeat, about what I had done in this world to find a god possible through poetry.

(Juan Ramon Jimenez)

It's possible, I read, for anyone to lead the contemplative life.
That we need but the briefest of moments.
A practice may be wedged into motherhood and work
balanced elegant
between the laundry and the combing out
of a daughter's matted curls.
And it is possible, it is.
There are side effects though
from attempting to answer two callings at once.
Like the bird in stutter-flight between two thoughts
at times utterly invisible—beyond invisible
and even the lark, in its anguish and joy
doesn't know if it will reappear, if it will sing.

I repeat, I'm choosing how to fail or at least
I'm learning to choose, let's begin there.
That much closer to enlightenment.
I'm a thousand lifetimes away, more.
I can almost see now the vast architecture
the grandeur of the city of interruptions.

One morning I'm consumed by love
and that afternoon, *consumed* by love.
Always somewhere between burning and burned out
until neither one is what it could be.
The two loves become confused, and I, bewildered.
So that when I give my full attention to the one
it turns into the other.
Whatever I've given birth to, I love like a mother
and when I'm mothering
I can't stop seeing the unruly poetry in her.

Then, I ask, what have I done in this world?
I'm learning to suspend myself, invisible, to stutter
into the dust between worlds
and I don't know anything at all by now, not yet
which feels almost like progress, a helpless sort of progress.

Every day I have more sympathy for the woman
sawed in two by a disenchanted magician
She sees her legs spun around, apart from her, a swirling star.
But all she thinks about is the sawdust
resplendent on the floor, out of her sight-line.
She smiles though with all her might
and when she's put back together
we know that her smile then is an angry one
exhausted, plastered on
and when everyone in the audience is wondering
how the illusion is accomplished
is it real or is it not?
she's wondering, limber, how to get the sawdust back, unseen.

As for me, I'm trying to find a god possible through poetry
I'm trying to relinquish, content, at peace
all the fine stardust I cup in my hands.

Sway

After weeks lost in the too shallow ardourless labyrinth
I want to come to the scene of the bonfire imperfectly.

It was a circuitous path and you might as well humor me
try and follow.
(Here I'm addressing my inward breath).

Weeks calling out unspeakable things
and then twice.
Once while eating dry bread
and then once cleaning the house while it rained
listening to Gould's *Goldberg Variations* and
the clean notes of rain, each regardless of each.
There was a flower inside me that wanted to open
and almost, it almost did.
It understood something
about time
about living.
This is when
I began to feel the swaying
a deep easy *sway*
reflecting obsolete italicized meanings of the word.
The stance
not quite human
and yet prepared, unflaunting.

Now is where I stop to read *The Stream of Life*
for courage though courage shouldn't be needed.
Later when I'm through making these notations
and I allow myself to breathe outwardly as well
then I'll take up that book and put it on my easel
and paint the cover red, many coats, until the red vision appears.

For now I'm trying to record what happens during several weeks
when one has lost one's nerve.

I began to sway and to direct my breathing inwardly.

When the rain tapered off
there were frogs
all the way from my childhood
and I could hear them all the way into my dreams
huddled in my bed every night.

Last night we took outside gin and tonics, stacks of books
and I sat on the side of the table by the Russian sage
and watched the bees become intoxicated, and occasionally
read a line of Akhmatova.

I am usually careful not to ask for things when I'm looking
up at the heavens
but I did ask.

The sounds of my adulthood
the racing of cars and motorcycles
were interfering with the sounds of my childhood.
The frogs, chirping and then that bird
whose song rises up twirling from the frog song.
I know the notes exactly only when it sings
and after I can't play it in my head
and so I'll never find a name for it.

What I asked.
Just one night before the end
to be lightly covered, in a bed of purest comfort
beneath a huge window
and no traffic and no sounds of other people
only the sound of everyone I love, in one house
breathing, all softness.

But what I really was asking
was for a particular night.
It was after the bonfire.
(Now you can discern the smoke perfume my hair
spread out on the pillow
now you can see the fire reflected in my damp eyes).

It was a work of art
the myriad sticks and logs, twigs and dried branches.
It was the bonfire
the one after the old tree nearly fell through the cedar cabin.
Half the summer spent clearing out the old and dead
and bunching it, fretting and weaving it into a pyramid
several times taller than I was then.

Half the summer left
the sun gone down just as it did last night
when we had to go in to see the words on the page.
It was time.
The paper was stuffed into the sculpture
and then gasoline poured.
Standing far back now, apart
the match thrown in.

And I am thrown
from the twilight into the dark
and back into a blaze of light.
I watched, my back on a young tree, swaying, serene.
How long did we watch, rapt?
I don't remember going inside
don't remember falling into bed
the rough sheets on skin
the way the bed felt like a hammock under the stars
that I could see with my eyes closed
while the frogs chirped and the beautiful maddening bird
with no name unwound its song into me
and I fell asleep
having been that close to, singed by
what then, too, would have been without name
the divine.

Dream Stumbling

While I combed out my daughter's hair
she said she'd had a dream that she'd had before
it was yet dark outside, and her hair yet held the dream scent.
And I forgot hers while I mused upon
mine which was about riding a gray horse
whose very grayness seemed significant.
The horse was recalcitrant—
this might even have been its name—
and overly weighed down, poorly loaded, unbalanced
so that it couldn't be said to have been its fault.
That it didn't wish to enter the forest.
That it kept stumbling over the hidden wish of the dream
to return to the place of the beforehand.

When she was safely at school—
all the way at the beginning of grade one
I went out walking
aching for her
I went out daydreaming
asked myself, what colour is a spark?
and answered, the colour of a blink, white light.
I was trying to remember things that I've never known
as though they had merely slipped my mind.

It happened then, though once I'd given it up, maybe twice
again I began yearning for my forest, the forest of my childhood
the greenest forest.
How could I have thought that the black hole in my chest
could be given up?

By lunchtime a new yearning
from out of and then folded back into the old one.
You see I began remembering how as a child
I could both lose myself and become lost in the true forest
fluid, for several minutes at a time
nothing was familiar and I had no idea where home was, what direction.
Too soon I would recognize a tree, oddly shaped, or some deadfall.
And then resume stumbling toward the known.

So now it is almost time for me to retrieve my daughter from school
and I yearn for a poem that would come to me, lost, punctual
requiring that it never be vocalized
that's how full of grace it would be
living only in the quiet of mouth-cave, breath.

All day long, dream stumbling
wanting to remember what it is to be without yearning
to be lost in the beyond of myself.
Wanting so badly a graceful poem, a quiet thing to hold
strands to gently comb through
I wanted to breathe in the lilac swoon of dreams
at the expense of forgetting the heaviness of daughter-yearning.

When night comes we will all of us
stumble again into dreams.
To my book of yearning
I shall add yearning for the silk gray recalcitrant horse
so I may adjust its load
which I see now was not heavy
so much as ill-balanced.
I see now it won't enter the forest
without the weight on its back
the dear weight.

A person of true grace would have known so much more
than I
before the end
of the first stanza
before the knots had been smoothed.
But O!
(are we not always in the beforehand?)
let me believe I stumble, raw-kneed
toward grace.

The Voices Culminate

The voices culminate in this good shower of rain
on the edge of another brief enormous summer.
Can summer contain all this?
The voices accumulate, they chant, Gregorian:
hang fire, steal fire, failure.
Voices battle, in this, my prayer to silence.

★

Poetry, says a voice, is just another
one of the names.

★

The view out my window
raindrops
low gray clouds
trees bending
one of them will break.
Another voice,
whatsoever is truly whole
has once been broken.

★

That we are responsible to the atom.
Write Antonia, write, and do not waste time!

★

And this shall be a target
unfolded
briefly
and I will await the arrows
feathered kindling.

(Later, sift through my smoldering
puzzle over so many perfect arrowheads).

★

I don't deny that I'm a counterfeit
a mere daydreamer.
If I have to
(I have to)
I'll steal
fire.

*

I submit at last to longing.
I'm growing my hair long again
so I may wear it as a braided necklace
I'm growing my hair long again
for my own sake.
I'm learning how to live.
I'm doing this for you
that I may gain the secret and give it to you
as I would bring in a bouquet of dahlias
petals still warm
in the middle of summer
place them on the kitchen table and walk away
into the quiet.

*

Every summer the web of voices
is thicker.
I live in a blaze of voices
never alone.
Walking, it's Walt Whitman.
And sitting in the backyard, Charles Wright.
In the red velvet chair, folding,
unfolding, on fire, Phyllis Webb.
When everyone is gone, Dahlia Ravikovitch.
A tear drops onto a handwritten page, Amichai.
Cloud watching, Annie Dillard.
Star gazing, Clarice Lispector.

And so on.

*

These scant fragments
are tinder-dry.

★

I am responsible to the atom
to the atom alone.

Lately I have begun noticing little fires.
All along they were there.
I've been following a path.
Candles, incense burning.
Small piles of kindling and then
fires, consuming, wild, and secret.

★

The voices culminate in this good shower of rain.
I dissolve
these substances I have become
retreat into other substances
stream powerless into the edges
of what we'll agree to call summer
but what is only the briefest of moments.
An atom.
The fire voices and the arrow voices
subside.
I only hear rain
or
the sounds from the scriptorium.

★

There, ink is fire.

★

All of this rain and yet
I am unquenched.

★

Fire is a magnanimous refuge, almost banal in its greatness
its dangerous phrasing
for which I am constantly homesick.
It is my business to be homesick, unquenched.
Unfolded no more.

Red Velvet Forest

Dream of the Red Forest

After three weeks of trying to capture the dream
I've left off.
Failed to weave it into my skin
and it has slipped from me thread by gossamer thread.
It was a week, you see, before I had a chance to write it down.
I've marked my diary with a red ribbon
those illegible pages.

The dream is the calling that I cannot answer.
But it is also, I discovered this a mere ten minutes ago
(do I keep discovering this?)
my calling to be quiet. To feel quiet.

Pining for my dream of the red forest
I'm going to write down everything
I have been this one morning
and there is only one hour left.
I came out into the backyard
affectionately I call it my paradise
I'm able to because the apple trees haven't yet any fruit.
It's the end of June 2004.
I've come outside with a great hunger in my belly.
Deliberately I have limited myself to coffee.

I want to be a recluse
wander in the desert.
I have a thirst for what cannot be and so
I water green into being.
I water honeysuckle vine, the wooly thyme, the lavender.

The grass I water and water because then it sparkles for me
like emeralds in the sun.
Did I mention the perfect blue of the sky? Clear.
I water the spider webs too, the one on the railing
the one on the swing-set
so that they too can become jewels in the green castle.

There's less than an hour left.
And I haven't even gotten to forgetting the dream.
Which is why it seems crucial to capture the morning.
Are they not each as elusive? as fleeting? as maddeningly forgettable?
Which illusion is more convincing?
The dream, the garden, the poem?

The petals from the black pansies have released
and skitter along the brick patio before my sandaled feet
(who would buy black flowers?) like burnt butterfly wings.

I thought once that I should like to sit in bars and cafes
and talk smokily about poetry.
Now I don't think poetry should be spoken about.
Rather we should write letters to each other on the subject.
The only way to get in is to be perfectly quiet.
Let's sit here and listen to our breathing.
Anything else will disturb what is almost happening.

A blue butterfly just flew across the arc of the sprinkler.
I should have my camera ready for such moments.

All the flowers are in the almost state—
peonies, lilies, Siberian irises.
Only the Oriental poppies begin to gape
flimsy red and pink and white negligees
reveal their black gorgeous souls.

When I was a child I could think without words.
I have the distinct memory of saying to myself,
you must remember how to do this for when you are older.
And now that's the only bit I can remember,
the saying to myself.

That's all this wants to be, then. And can't.

And so I will tell you about the dream of the red forest.
Let me first muster courage to turn
to the illegible beribboned pages in my diary
and attempt to decipher what I'd written.

I dreamed that I traveled into a particular book
and the book was both a castle and
a forest and both were red.
The only colour in the dream was red.
Illegible.
Illegible.
When I woke up my shoulder blades hurt.
(Two days later, I see flipping ahead, they still hurt).
My head had been shaved.
But miraculously my hair had also grown back.
I had gone somewhere and come back.
The rest, illegible. Illegible. Illegible.

Velvet Fire, Tranquil Blue

The week that Picasso's blue boy fetched a record price at auction
we waited on proverbial pins and needles
for a word
on a year's worth of paintings hanging
in a show half a country away.
And it's true, not only pins, there must be needles as well.

We're adept at appearing calm and unfazed by now.
Every morning for a week we drink coffee and read our horoscopes
and are tranquilized.
We awake to brazen snow sprawled sheer on the roofs in May
and shrug, blinking.

What is this life then, that we never can quite reckon?
One minute I'm filled with fear, easily filled.
But maybe that's just acting, too, a game I play with myself.
And then I'm fearless for at least a day
after getting the mail
and that one small, good piece of news
even if it's not quite the news we were waiting on.

All week I open my vials of aromatherapy
cinnamon, then vanilla, and then cinnamon again.
I harbor an atavistic urge to light fires
first to keep the yellow eyes away
and then to kindle in my soul
what had been intrinsic
and now has become remote, clouded over.

When I was young, on the farm, we were given matches
to light fires in the burning barrel down by the barn
those nights when the mosquitoes were heavy in the sky.
I remember playing with matches
experimenting with fire, practicing
with dry things, brittle things.
Seeing how long these would take to catch.
And when the fire blazed I would jab with a stick
at the chapped, scorched sides
of the barrel where it had become another substance
half metal, half skin of the fire.
Reluctantly then, I sprinkled grass on the flames
the smoke always a surprise
mesmerized by the velvet fire
I never moved back soon enough
when the smoke came to fold itself
into corners of eyes, sharp into nostrils.

I know this life to be boundless
but also
the fire keeps no one and nothing away.
I'm collecting matches anyway
I'll be wreathed by the velvet fire
its tranquil blue
if nothing else,
let me be changed, sharp, and stung deep and calm by this life.

Insomnia Diary

In the living room at four thirty a.m.
I watched the coming of the light.
It is my destiny, at intervals to awake early
utterly alone, utterly quiet
near shattered.
Later, when the sun buries my fleeting thoughts
it is also my sad destiny to seem otherwise.
For now, I am busy watching an uninhibited awakening
the beautiful half light coming into being.
I must be here to realize my failings.
My epitaph: she failed in essential matters.
But before I put that into use
I need to rewrite the definition of failure.

This entry proof these diaries are for me alone.
For I believe in the undivulged.
It is too easy to pour the soul steady into, now, five a.m.
that mud vessel with its slow leak.
Oh, what am I?
What creature? what failed creature am I?
There, at last a truth, in the form of a question.
Faithfully have I failed.

I'm so tired and yet irretrievably awake.
I should be reading poetry
rather than making a fool of myself to myself.
For that is all this can be.
And if I overindulge
it is because of the extreme comfort of writing by hand
the flow which means precisely nothing.

My existence, truly, is all comfort.
I hardly know suffering.
I'm sure I've made up every short angle of my suffering.
But this tack must be ended or it will be the end of me.

What woke me—
I became a figure in a painting
and I knew that to attempt anything after having been this figure
was absurd.
The painting: *The Red Vision* by Leonor Fini.
A room with two doors, two windows, three figures.
One shadow woman, through a door, her back to the viewer
she looks out the window.
At the threshold of the same door
a girl, whitened, in a nightdress, an apparition?
She looks up, one hand writing in air.
Then, near the ceiling, as though having leapt through the far door
the red vision.
A woman, flame or flower? a fireball.
And now it is left for you to decide which figure dreamed me
which figure I dreamed I had become.

I sit here on the edge of this earthbound couch
adorned, cold.
A fraud, a fraud, a coward.
I know what I am meant to give.
Poetry, you see, wants only this:
nakedness.
And when you give
it kills you
with its one adorable sting.
So for now
I will play the fool the coward the fraud
Scheherazading
I will dance the dance of veils
employ sleight of hand, tricks with mirrors
anything at my disposal.

If I goad it, confess to it the fine edge of my sins
the hellish clemency of insomnia
might some day deliver my own secondhand red vision
its doors and windows all at exactly the right perspective
but look how tired I am.
And a whole long day, its glazed din, to get through.
I can hardly contemplate the sun, old rasping ball of fire
the way it rests weak
low
on the rooftops.

The Forest of Disappearance

It wouldn't make sense, the red forest
I would paint layer upon layer
time upon time
if I could paint
my dreams.

Who's there, over your shoulder?
There's the sense of thick fabric
a lurking brocade or sly velvet.
Your back is in the painting, inexplicably.

What else? At first the sounds make you duck your head.
But when you find the path it begins.
You feel yourself disappearing, actually feel
a sensation of erasure, or rather, of being painted
over.

You walk on the packed red earth
past red birch trees, cherry trees with fruit
like bleeding hearts
the red hummingbirds carry off in pieces
rabbits, lady's slippers, dagger
just as in the story children tell.
Only here you crave the taste of the dagger.

Red bells and red tigers, strawberries edge the path
that leads to a small fire
housed in a nest of twigs and moss.

Remember, this is a painting.
And the flames are merely a fleck of paint
a flick of the wrist.
When you look closely
they could be read as a bird or leaves.
Farther away though, clearly,
they disappear.

But how does a dream end in a painting?
Right before you turn to leave, you come upon the velvet jacket
hanging from a tree branch
and you understand all along
to whom it belonged
and just as quickly lose
understanding.

Burning Forest

All this week I sat in the backyard minding children
unworried under the haze
of forest fires a province away.

Today I sit inside while it rains. I hold nothing.
Hold nothing back.

If it weren't for my copy of Rumi
with all the underlined passages
and if it weren't for the dog-eared pages
of art books
showing me the various pleasing colours of angel's wings
I'm sure I would have wept
all this morning
holding my nothing
so carefully, after all.

They should be colourless, shouldn't they, the wings?

Rumi's falcon dives into the forest
and surrenders
abandons the sky.

Maybe it's as far off as British Columbia
but some day I'm going to learn the language of flames
even if I can only think it and never speak.
Quiet, I'm going to clothe myself in serenity
and when I dive, slow, slow, and colourless, into the burning forest
I'm going to carry the knowledge of rain
and the tender despairing remembrance
of holding nothing.

The Red Tree, My heart

Part of the answer
is that I'm too fragile after all.

I walked out yesterday
off the gravel path and through the gate
into the utilities corridor
all of that energy strung out above
and to the west of where I walked.
Most of summer the gate was closed
but now it was slung open
and a path had already been tramped toward the trees.

A thin stand of trees, adrift
maybe once it was a windbreak for a farmhouse
well before the city infringed.

Walking toward, it seemed there was the skin
of a red house or an outbuilding just on the other side
a sign the narrow forest had once belonged
to someone, and even to someone's heart.
But drawing nearer it revealed itself as a tree
quietly and gently
a red voice in the still green forest of early autumn.

I walked then to the other side
where the tree, which had seemed so vulnerable
was hidden from view.
Instead I saw a tree house, ladderless, precarious
quite high.
Had it been finished rather than just having a floor
there would have been two rooms.
One, a near square, opening up to
the other, the shape of a fan—crude wing
specimen pinned down and held up to sky.
It was what it was mostly because of the randomness of trees
and availability of scrap lumber.

And then there was my blithe encounter with the butterfly
which kept flying upward along one tree trunk and then back down
as though it were tracing an invisible ladder.
After this, I couldn't stay long but felt I had to flee this place.

The rest of the answer is the red tree, my heart.
The rest of the answer is the red tree, my wingless state, and
the slung, scrap beauty of the underbelly.

Red

I'm too far away from
or I've been swallowed by
the forest.

I've spent three days deciding which of these rings true.

I'd have the answer
if I could only remember the feeling
the way the forest at nightfall
leaks top down colour
drains itself
presumably it all returns to the roots
the last colour to leave is of course
red
and that colour seeps a little into every being
who wants
it.

This is when you look at the forest, steeped, and think
black
but feel
see
red.

The third possibility.
I've swallowed the nocturnal forest
and am now too far away.

Circling the Forest

As a child I was deep
and for a while deeper
in the book of the forest
knowing with precision wordlessness
and entwined with lion's breath.

It occurs to me this morning, after many mornings
of walking out through the gate and out to the narrow forest
and merely walking the length of it and then back—
that one may go all around, circling.
I pick my ceremonial piece of wild grass
and twirl it in my fingers
all the while tasting a shy sweetness
I want to call enchantment.

The cryptogram of the leaves
first comes back to me.
The ever-changing message in the orderly turning.
At the edge, the wild roses
their fiery red-orange leaves
and the fierce blush of rosehips
bring me back
and this is where I momentarily
remember the sweet breath of falling
into what I want to call enchantment.

But did I fall or was I felled?
The answer is that this forest is thinned, it is thinned, a sliver of itself.
And yet it is, itself, a forest and I
am thinned out by it.

A surge of happiness
I looked so deeply into the trees—
this was once second nature—
that I am one of them
and all the thousands of shapes and colours and textures
I remember them by breath
have breathed them into me
my soul aligned to forest.

I was this morning as a tree walking, circling
breathing in the indecipherable messages.
I was in deep, circling at an adjacent, previously unknown depth.
I was calling and calling with each lion-ish breath
and with a great and childish want, enchantment.

The Azure-Vermilion Tangle

The one thing that mustn't slip away does so.
I come back to the birthing scene only as a milk angel would
distorted high up in a domed ceiling, robed in Madonna blue
almost swallowed up by loose, back-breaking fresco passages
of beings winging and billowing across a prettily clouded cerulean sky.

In a mere six years what have I not forgotten?
A babe is placed on my chest
there—amidst the noise of the world, the most perfect quiet of my life
joy is henceforth measured
against this unwinding
the self soaring from the self.
A little later, unwound, her blue eyes bleating into mine
must be when I was transformed, unwounded,
whole, and shattered.
Then the flooding knowledge and the red clarity
like walking with closed eyes
the sun streaming in like the beginning
and the sudden possession of an exquisite velveted fearlessness.

But lives come in and out of the world at breakneck speed
each one slips from us, colours fade and chip away
the lived-in years are as a thin murky film.

*

In the fourteenth century a recipe is set down for making the colour azure
which in fact results in vermilion.
In spite of this detour, known as *The Azure-Vermilion Tangle*
the recipe persists for several hundred years
with little to no comment.

How to say what happens after mortar and pestle, oil and flask
the blinking, breathtaking jolt of discovery
when blue is red.

Often, it seems that one moves from expectation
into the unutterable existence of what is.
I've so often said *azure* when what I meant was *vermilion*
or more accurately the one becomes tangled in the other
each one changing how the other is seen
and in the end all I can do is pray to keep both words
in my mouth at one time, to give myself to them, open.

So even now I understand the recipe less as error than gift
making the pain of being aloft, separated from my own fearless soaring
that much more bearable.

Red Velvet

It came into our possession
the abandoned red velvet dress
and later came to be the subject of a painting
that now hangs in our bedroom
across from its companion piece
the heaped white silk.

The painting, with its deep shadowed valleys, bright peaks
the creases and crumples
is more landscape than still life.

I don't like to draw attention to a seeming expansiveness.

I don't like to think of Medea
her dress of fire.

There is a hint of where the bodice was stitched.
There is the slightest hint of sleeve, skirt.

Other things were abandoned as well.
A tiered cake, flower girls, music, winter dreams.

I like to think of Medea
that dress of fire.

Maybe if the painting had been called
Medea's Gift, or *Burning Dress*
maybe then it would have sold.
But that's not the way still life paintings are named.
They're named in the way articles
belonging to the dead are named.
Bequeathed formal, itemized, descriptive.

I was never told the true name of the bride
or how many bridesmaids there were to be
all dressed one January in red velvet.
And the painting keeps the fullness of its truth
with an absence of ceremony
mysteriously and with respect.

The dress has nothing to do with Medea.
But remember the seventh swan in the fairy tale?
His sister knit all her swan-brothers sweaters from nettles
but the last one not quite finished
when she had to throw it over him
and he was left with one aching wing as a result.

I've wanted to burn completely.

And yet, I'm wed to the unresolved wing of the swan and
I'm bequeathed to the silent soliloquy of red velvet.

There are so many ways to burn.

A Way of Meeting

The precise reason for doing this?
The idea came from a cowboys and Indians movie
squinted at instead of a nap
maybe home sick from school.

You do it to sneak up on someone in the forest.
Is it the enemy? a friend?
The plot may hinge on this.
But I knew that being able to do this
in real life
would mean something else
that hadn't to do with another human
hadn't to do with that sort of survival.
Learning to walk without sound
meant that one had reached another depth—
another ring inward—of forest-knowing.
A way of meeting the teeth in the shadows
escorted by quiet.

It's an odd betrayal to relate this memory
so embedded as it is.
A betrayal of child-thought
how as a child I knew my adult self
wouldn't quite understand how I thought
how I felt and thought together these kinds of things
how the two were inextricably braided.

I knew I would forget nuances
what I meant by
the teeth in the shadow
I knew I would forget the unsurrounded panting
the love rising up and clear of the shadow.
How it would be, in that way, lost
detached, into mute air
not even taken by surprise.

Want

I might still call this
the last forest poem.
Or I might name it after
small needs.

I went to my remnant forest after rain
and staggered painfully about in its fringe perfume
which is mostly remembered perfume.
This is what I have.
Is what I will want.
And want.

The leaves mostly gone now
I can see through to the other side
I can see all the way to the opposite end of the field
in the utilities corridor
to the other remnant forest (the lesser one because not mine).
The wind blew away the leaves
and it blew nearly away the sound of the traffic.
The highway is so close you know I could call for help
and someone might come.

I haven't had time to go to the other forest
(it seems incredible that once, they met)
because I am responsible to this remnant
and to the drama that daily unfolds.

Every day another tree has been cut through
new lumber has arrived.
Things have been built.
Fires have been made and let to go out.
Today a pile of rosebushes heaped
beside the fallen tree which has been made into a balance beam—
two by four like a spine nailed to it every inch or so.

There are two tree houses now
where before there was only one.
The second house had two stories
and then the next day one level was on the ground.

I wouldn't try to interpret the drama.
It's enough to balance oneself, staggering in the perfume
of what will some day be another's yearning
another's lost home.
Fine agony.

Dragonsblood Red

I dedicate myself
to the grip of the dragon
the meat and muscle of it
I dedicate myself to the dragon
whose tail bindeth and spanneth
and I dedicate myself to the fallen elephant
who buyeth it full sore
and to his weight full and bearing down
and I dedicate myself to each
because each slayeth each.

I delicate myself
to the mingling of their blood
and to all the ground that soaks it
thereafter speaking cinnabar
and I delicate myself
to the elephant who is left out of all naming
and at the last
I must delicate myself
as others have
as others do
as others will
to the color red
even though
I am sometimes not at all sure that we do not pay too dear.
(No, I must revise, it's worth
every drop).

To the Wolf

Wolf I scarcely know you
your namelessness
though by some you have been called
the kid.

Do you remember me?
Once long ago I went into that forest repeatedly
deep alone
usually barehanded
but occasionally with a pretty blue child's bow
and real pheasant feathered arrows.
And with a small French poodle
you could have eaten in one flash
of your lovely yellow teeth
but didn't.
By another's hand the bow once killed
a squirrel and there were tears
but not mine
I laughed
couldn't help.

Wolf, I want you now.
I won't sail arrows into your softness
and you won't swallow me.
Swallow me.

I see you loping always aslant aslant low and shadowed.
I don't know anything about you dear wolf.
Will you come to my grown-up door
to my city house?
I hear your footsteps in the snow
though you leave no tracks
and I'm afraid of your glimmerings.
I know you come disguised to doors
your floured paw, your honeyed throat.
When I sing are you not the accompanist?
Oh God, wolf, tell me
when will you arrive?

I tell you I'm afraid
will not you come?
I tell you I'm not
love my fear.

You know all my disguises
my velvet cloaks and my jeweled masks
and my tall boots and my crimson lips
and all the others too.

But I come to you clean wolf and plain
and low aslant and aslant
and the least you can do is tell me why
say your name quiet as breath.
Though it's true and nonsense
I don't want a name
just breath.

A Third

-after reading Marina Tsvetaeva's 'Two Forest Kings'

It wasn't a dream I was dreaming.
I was let go into dream by the forest king
which is how the forest king lets go.

Marina, I might rather keep this scene
where I did no such thing as resist.

I heard him say,
"I love you. I am stung by your beauty"
and I knew just what that meant
the words behind that drape of words.

I was small, my hair was easily white as snow
and I wore a purple woolen hat that day
I leaned against my father's back, safely against
his strength, his warmth.
He was skimming the arctic cat over the snow
so fast and then he slowed to ask
are you afraid? no. to go faster? no
as fast as fast can go? and you won't tell? no.

How far from home we'd gone down that cut-line
edged as it was by gray willows
snow endless ahead and trees thick on either side
but now we turned to home and rode
on our own clouded tracks
in the late gray of the afternoon.
The cat opened up and in the high thrill
and in the purring I heard the forest king speak.
Whispers before had I known
but these were words and I nodded
there was—you know the story—no choice.

Oh, the narrow escape is never an accident.
It hurt, too, maybe more than being taken.
The glittering and the shuddering
opposed to all that warmth.

When did I fall asleep? and when did we slow?
My cheeks were white circles but they didn't sting
until I was by the grand fire
and remembering the dreamwords
henceforth you will be stung cold and white by beauty
and that is how you will know my love.

Sorrow, at Last, Failure. Joy.

Because the approach matters I come to this
through the beforehand of a catnap.
You see, the couch beckons me
I've just witnessed the long absent sun
ease its thick ray
from out of the snow blue sky
onto my very own comfortable spot.
And I want so terribly to curl up there and forget.

It matters, that this is merely an approach.
Better: a mere approach.

⋆

Last year in the backyard I burned a copy of my own book
and it has been burning ever since.
There was a truth in that moment of the burning book
and I've been trying to say it to myself
but it includes such a haze of smoke and a dampness.

It was a day exposed to silence
when I clicked the lighter and knelt
in the smudged crystal snow of spring
on the sighing earth not quite frozen
and willed the reluctant thing to ignite
riffling the dry pages
praying that it would
burst forth
into flame.

Slowly, then, it burned.
Through my own breath visible in the air above
did I see it
blacken and curl and take on the appearance
of a log in some hearth, warming and fine and aglow.
I saw words appear and disappear—
the flames licked and ate and licked and swallowed—
like a kind spell
rewarding sorrow with a softer sorrow.

At last, failure.
Joy.

It hurts to relive
not only because my fingers were singed
when I reached into the low flames to turn pages
or because my knees were sore and soaked through
from kneeling long in last year's frozen green.

It hurts because of what I must ask you
because of what you must do.
Ah, but I see you already know
(and how did you know?)
in your innocence to ask
the question
the very question that was not to be asked?

You also know what must be written with these
so here is your box of redbird matches
and here is my book
and here, you know the stakes.

The sparkling orange is yours too
and the heart which ever after firmly holds in its palm
abandoned, most ordinary, flames.

But, the truth?

I know what it is to break, to fall apart
into the fire's flickering loneliness
and into dimensions of sorrow
hollow as hunger and stripped down so far
that I'm invisible.
I know what it is to resolve myself in the flames.
I know how to take from ashes what belongs to me.

*

It is only now
because of a *you*
that I make my way to the sun
to curl up in my exhaustion and dimmed failure
with such joy.

Woodcutter in the Forest

-after re-reading John Berger's "Seker Ahmet and the Forest"

How small the axe
and how large the love of the tree
that looms into the gold-ash clearing
casting its shadow toward the donkey's burden
and his woodcutter.

I can hear the conversation in that perfect rustling silence
so very great.
I am engaged by the adoration
of the one swallowed
for the one
striking out, brimming over
and also, more so
the reciprocal adoration.

After listening a while
I sink into
alone
drawing it close to me
the rosy warmth of silence.

★

The painting is only an instant.

I don't paint, either
but I want to go and meet the adoration
in the quiet color.

And this is how I will take my leave
into the vast instant of paint.

When I was the Forest

At the end of a book, even a book one has written, it is cast aside. Shrugged onto a night table, or dropped from the end of fingers, broken-hinged, to the foot of the armchair. Other books come to rest against or on top of it. Dust arrives. The book remains though, however lost, and one might as well write a love letter. To the book? or to whom one was while writing it?—to whom one became?—or to the state of becoming? Or maybe just to remembering, if it is possible to write a love letter to the act of remembering.

Maybe this is a love letter to loose ends, the ones left over after a book, that never want quite to be tied up. And then there are the bits and pieces that find you afterwards—words from other poets, in this case, that arrive as signs, if you will, a magical affirmation. There are also the small stones, gifts, let's call them poems, that were there all during, jangled and smoothed in the palm of the hand, in pockets, that never explicitly revealed themselves or were never tossed down on the forest path.

⋆ ⋆ ⋆

A silence has entered me after this book of the red velvet forest, unlike the silences I have known after other books. I can't help thinking of that magic of being seen and not heard. A magic command, this was not an admonishment I minded as a child. In fact, I'm convinced it was always said to me, a notoriously quiet child, as a joke, or at least I took it as one. There is some connection to the quietness I now feel entering me, and the quiet that children know as a terrain (dare I say, forest?). Rumi said, "This is how it always is / when I finish a poem. / A great silence overcomes me, / and I wonder why I ever thought / to use language." This is part of it, too. It is the silence before all that resides outside language, before the invisibly coloured perfume that wafts about and surrounds language. There is the kind of thinking that children do before they have a vocabulary for all that they see and experience and hear. I'm interested in remembering the deep-within-ness of this type of thinking, though, really, it's scarcely possible. Every time I try, the memory of being able to do this swims away like a dream at the alarm clock.

Still, I believe this kind of child-thinking is at the core of poetic thinking and it's why I'm drawn to dreams. Marina Tsvetaeva talks about magical words, words that are "magical apart from their meanings, physically magical." These words, she says, "do not require comprehension, only hearing..."

They come from the "child's dream language." For Tsvetaeva, the magic word from that dream language, discovered when she was seven years old, was "the Pathfinder." The Pathfinder was "the miracle into which the child and the poet walk without thinking as if walking home..." For me, the word was simply "clearing" and sometimes, just "forest." But the one held the other and both were dream words, magic words.

"What in earliest childhood is made your own—is your own once and for all." This, too, is Tsvetaeva. The forest, the clearing, is where I walk toward without thinking. That forest, my particular forest, which in all likelihood would be unrecognizable to me were I to enter it today, in its present state, is, even so, once and for all, my own. I like that Tsvetaeva says, once and for all. It is a fairytale phrase, "once and for all." And yet, I lose the forest, have lost it, given it up. I've exchanged it for other magic words, or so I have thought. It arrives again.

* * *

This afternoon—it's early November—the weather was fine enough for a walk out. The ice was melting from the sidewalk. I walked out to the path I have walked for two years in between writing poems, sometimes during. The path is one part gumbo, one part ice today. I walked toward my makeshift forest, my pretend forest. It's not a forest at all today, with all the forest poems I can write, for the moment, written. Sad thing! Already, the forest is different. Scarcely four trees deep, it is both impenetrable and impossibly scant. But, oh, still beautiful, for lack of a better word, I call it beautiful. It seems doomed. Certainly there is little chance that it will be anything more than what it is.

The forest, this not-forest, seems to me, different. How? Returned to itself? Indifferent? Possessing a greater silence? A lesser one? The cars on the nearby freeway are an ever-increasing hum. More junk seems to make its way here every time I come out to meet it. Why do I care anyhow? This is not my once-and-for-all forest but a mere shadow or echo or fringe. Then why did I sing to it in my head upon approach, all this fall, a pop song, sung by Sheryl Crow, with the lines, "It's not having what you want, it's wanting what you've got." After reading my manuscript, with these lines in the epigraph, a friend said she'd read the same in an altered form. In a book called *The Essential Mystics*, there are the lines by Rabban Gamliel, "Desire only that which has already been given. / Want only that which you already have."

* * *

When I was a child, wandering, as I did those many mornings and afternoons in the forest, I made a pact with a fairy, or maybe it was only myself, but I did certainly make a pact to write a story some day when I was grown up about all those forest things that do not require comprehension. The fairies, you see, lived at the far end of our eighty acres property where there was a cut-line and therefore a long line of trees and bush and clumps of root and soil piled up. It was something like a tipi, but only in that at intervals there were what seemed to be abodes, where the trees had been shoved together at the top to form an upside down V. And the fairies sometimes lived in amongst the uprooted trees and behind the pockets of moss and shimmering goldish-brown leaves that hung down from the deadened branches. They lived in the deep within. Sometimes they lived in the clearings which were often moved.

The goal, not that I entertained thoughts of any goal, or could have spoken it, was the clearing. One walked into the forest to find the clearing. To find it one also had to enter a dream-like state, lost. And to walk without sound. There were many rules. Did the fairies tell them to me, or does a child know the rules of the forest? You must touch a certain number of trees, chew a certain type of grass. You must become forest.

If you asked me then, would I have said I believed in forest fairies? I don't think so. Could I have told you of the promise I had made? To the forest, to the fairies. I'm not even quite getting at it now, of course. How could I? The pact was to write a certain kind of story, for children, to lead them to the forest. To lure them? And I only know now this feeling of having broken a promise. I feel broken-promised, promise-broken.

⋆ ⋆ ⋆

"When I was the Forest" is the title of a poem by Meister Eckhart. In Daniel Ladinsky's translation, it begins, "When I was the stream, when I was the / forest, when I was still the field, / when I was every hoof, foot, / fin and wing, when I / was the sky / itself / no one ever asked me did I have a purpose..." Another friend sent a copy of this poem to me after reading my Red Velvet Forest manuscript. It affected me so that all day I kept taking out the sheet with the poem and staring at it, not even reading it. The poem continues, "It was when we left all we once were that / the agony began, the fear and questions came, / and I wept, I wept. And tears / I had never known / before. / So I returned to the river, I returned to / the mountains. I asked for their hand in marriage again, / I begged to wed every object / and creature..."

This poem brought to me a great quiet, and silently I kept repeating the words, when I was the forest, when I was still the field, over and over throughout the course of that day. I felt these words, I knew these words, I felt I had traveled them, I was the forest, and the past tense hurt me each time I said them to myself. Saying these words, silently, reading them silently, led me to remember how I have always thought about my poems as primarily silent utterances. Much has been said about the oral nature of poetry and I don't discount any of it, but merely claim a sliver of space for a type of poetry that contains an inner silence, a hush, and asks first to be approached through silence, alone.

In her book, *Fifty Days of Solitude*, Doris Grumback tells of the Palayins of southern India. She says throughout their lives they "speak very little. By the age of forty they are silent. Those in their community who continue to speak are considered abnormal, 'their behaviour offensive.'" It strikes me that before this book reaches, as it is said, the light of day, I will have reached forty years of age. I don't imagine I will become as silent as a forty year old Palayin, but I do have hopes of having a further understanding by then, I have a year and a half to go, of this new terrain of silence that I have merely re-discovered and that goes on at all times. I remember now that the silence is from when I was the forest. When I was a child in the forest.

I said that this was a love letter, and I still think it is. To the child in the forest. To the incomprehensible dream language of that child. And to the silence wherein the language takes place.

Notes

One Night. This poem is to some degree in conversation with Rumi's poem, "The Night Air" (Coleman Barks, translator). Rumi talks about the open window between us, 'mixing the night air of our beings.' 'Mystics,' says Rumi, 'are experts in laziness.'

Alone, Alone, Alone, Together. Though Yehuda Amichai is one of my oft referred to poets, it was some time before I came to find the words again which had been imbedded in my subconscious. The lines, slightly different than I had remembered are from the poem "1924." They are, "And whoever remembers his childhood best / is the winner, / if there are any winners."

This Time. G.H. is the protagonist in Clarice Lispector's *The Passion According to G.H.*

Blue Girl. C.L. is Clarice Lispector. The line "each of us is responsible for the entire world" is from "Annunciation" which is in the volume titled *Selected Cronicas.*

Talisman. In an article called "The Destruction of the Book," Ian Donaldson notes that "To speak about the likelihood of one's book being used as waste paper may be in part a talismanic act, designed to ward off ill fortune and avert the result the writer most deeply fears."

The Voices Culminate. Lines by Phyllis Webb (from "Some Final Questions") were the starting point of this poem and it seems proper to gratefully acknowledge them here: "doubled up I feel / small like these poems / the area of attack / is diminished." Other unacknowledged voices that might be heard echoing in the poem are those of George Sand, Michelangelo, and the anonymous author of the *Cloud of Unknowing.*

Dream of the Red Forest. Though unnecessary to an understanding of the poem, readers may find it interesting to know that the book traveled into via dream was *Cave in the Snow*, the story of Tenzin Palmo. For purposes of meditation, Tenzin Palmo secluded herself in a cave in the Himalayas for twelve years beginning in the mid-1970s.

The Azure-Vermillion Tangle. Daniel Thompson describes the tangle in his book, *The Materials and Techniques of Medieval Painting*.

Dragonsblood Red. In the same volume noted above, Thompson quotes Bartholomew Anglicus' account of the epic battle between the elephants and dragons. Some of the phrases in the poem are lifted from Anglicus. It is Thompson who says, "I am sometimes not at all sure that we do not pay too dear for our scientific knowledge." An interesting aside: Cennino said of dragonsblood red, "Leave it alone for it is not of a condition to do you much honour."

To the Wolf. For inspiration, I am indebted to Helene Cixous' essay, "Love of the Wolf."

A Third. Marina Tsvetaeva's "Two Forest Kings" can be found in the book, *Marina Tsvetaeva, A Captive Spirt: Selected Prose*. The essay compares Goethe's "Erlkonig" with the version by the Russian writer Zhukovsky. The line "I love you. I am stung by your beauty!" is from Goethe's version. In Tsvetaeva's translation the text continues, "If you won't come by choice—I will take you by force!"

Woodcutter in the Forest. John Berger's essay on Seker Ahmet Pasa's painting "Woodcutter in the Forest" appears in his collection, *About Looking*. Berger says that "the attraction and the terror of the forest is that you see yourself in it as Jonah was in the whale's belly." He goes on to say, "Now this experience, which is that of anybody familiar with forests, depends upon your seeing yourself in double vision. You make your way through the forest and, simultaneously, you see yourself, as from the outside, swallowed by the forest." Though I've only seen the painting in reproduction, for me, the attraction outweighs the terror in this instance.

Bibliography

Amichai, Yehuda. *The Selected Poetry of Yehuda Amicahai.* Trans. Chana Bloch and Stephen Mitchell. Berkeley: U of California Press, 1986.

Berger, John. *About Looking.* New York: Pantheon, 1980.

Cixous, Helene. *Stigmata: Escaping Texts.* London: Routledge, 1998.

Donaldson, Ian. "The Destruction of the Book." *Book History* 1 (1998): 1-10.

Grumbach, Doris. *Fifty Days of Solitude.* Boston: Beacon Press, 1994.

Ladinsky, Daniel. *Love Poems from God.* New York: Penguin, 2002.

Lispector, Clarice. *The Passion According to G.H.* Trans. Ronald Sousa. Minneapolis: University of Minnesota Press, 1988.

Lispector, Clarice. *Selected Cronicas.* Trans. Giovanni Pontiero. New York: New Directions, 1984.

Rumi. *The Essential Rumi.* Trans. Coleman Barks. New York: Harper Collins, 1995.

Thompson, Daniel V. *The Materials and Techniques of Medieval Painting.* New York: Dover, 1956.

Tsvetaeva, Marina. *A Captive Spirit: Selected Prose.* Trans. J. Marin King. Ann Arbor, Michigan: Ardis, 1980.

Webb, Phyllis. *The Vision Tree: Selected Poems. Vancouver: Talon Books, 1982*